C1

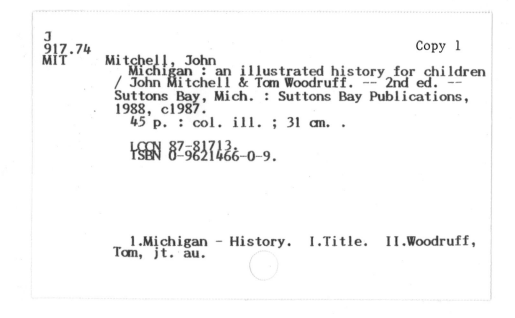

for Mary, Matt and Andrew

Suttons Bay Publications
301 St. Joseph Box 361
Suttons Bay, Michigan 49682

1st edition July 87
2nd edition Oct. 88

Printed and bound in Michigan
Library of Congress Catalog Card Number 87-81713
ISBN 0-9621466-0-9

MICHIGAN
AN ILLUSTRATED HISTORY FOR CHILDREN

John Mitchell & Tom Woodruff

Giant white pine trees once darkened the Michigan countryside. Indian hunters could travel the ancient forests for days without seeing the sun. Later, loggers found the tallest white pines by listening for the sound of the wind rushing through their highest branches.

But no matter how big, every white pine tree depends on its many tiny needles to keep it alive. Each needle colors and feeds and adds to the strength of the tree.

Michigan is like the white pine tree, with many different stories, each a pine needle. Together the stories give life to the special place called Michigan.

This is how Michigan looks today. The lakes that shape Michigan are so big they are called the Great Lakes.

Michigan is made up of two peninsulas. A peninsula is a piece of land surrounded on three sides by water. The Lower Peninsula is shaped like the back of your left hand. The Upper Peninsula is a long finger squeezed tight by water. Lake Superior, Michigan's northern border, is the largest lake in the world.

LAKE SUPERIOR

UPPER PENINSULA

LAKE MICHIGAN

LAKE HURON

LOWER PENINSULA

MICHIGAN

LAKE ERIE

The earth is a very old place which has changed many times. As part of the earth, Michigan was once very different than it is today.

A long time ago the earth was a scary place,
shaking with earthquakes and the fiery explosions
of volcanoes. There was no life, anywhere.

For millions of years the earth was hot and dry. Then heavy rains fell for centuries, creating the oceans.

Life on earth began in the oceans with tiny, one-celled creatures. Later, plants used the energy of the sun to make their own food. The oceans proved friendly to life. Plants and animals survived and over time became more complex, changing in shape and size.

Skeletons of some ancient plants and animals settled on the ocean floor. Sand and mud covered them and in time hardened into stone. The skeletons left pictures in the stone called fossils.

Fossils reveal a detailed picture of life found long ago in the oceans. The Petoskey stone is a well-known fossil from an ocean that once covered Michigan.

After many years some plants and animals moved from the oceans on to land. Soon the earth was green with ferns and tree-sized mosses and alive with the movement of many different animals.

Dinosaurs, the largest of land creatures, lived at this time. Some were as tall as trees and walked on four legs. Others used leathery wings to fly through the air. Some dinosaurs were gentle and ate only plants. A few had spiked teeth and ate anything they could catch!

Slowly the earth cooled. The changing climate caused most dinosaurs to die out and become extinct. Later big sheets of ice called glaciers spread over the land. In Michigan it was winter all year around.

Special animals called mammals were able to survive on a cool earth. Hair on their bodies helped to keep them warm. Young mammals developed inside their mothers, not in eggs laid in a nest or buried in the ground.

In time the earth warmed slightly and the glaciers retreated. Some of the water they left behind formed the five Great Lakes. Many different mammals, including the mastodon and the musk ox, moved into Michigan as the glaciers melted away.

Ten thousand years ago people began to roam the woods of Michigan.

People were able to use their brains to improve their lives. They made tools to work with and weapons for hunting. For warmth, they fashioned clothes from the skin of animals.

At night families huddled close to roaring fires and spoke of many adventures in the wild country.

People were always finding better ways to live. As the number of people on earth increased, they started to work together in tribes.

Early tribes in Michigan moved often in their search for food. Hunters armed with bow and arrow stalked elk in the dark forest. Other tribal members netted fish from lakes and rivers or gathered wild rice and berries.

For the early tribes, home was a place in the woods where the day's search for food ended.

The Indians were Michigan's first farmers. They grew corn and beans and other vegetables in fields near their round, bark-covered houses.

Farming changed the way the Indians lived. By planting and harvesting their own crops, the tribes were no longer forced to be on the move, always hunting for food. They could settle in one place.

In the safety of the settlement Indian artists had time to stitch a fancy pattern on a deer-skin dress or experiment with a design on pottery.

Most Indians living in Michigan in the year 1500 were descendants of the ancient Algonquin family. The three main tribes — the Ottawa, Chippewa, and Potawatomi — spoke a similiar language and shared religious beliefs. The tribes were known as the Three Fires.

At the time Michigan was a magnificent forest, filled with wild animals and roamed by the hunters of the Three Fires. The Indians took from the forest only what they needed for food and clothes. Nature quickly replaced what they used.

The many lakes and rivers of Michigan were natural paths for the Indians to travel. So they built birch-bark canoes strong enough to ride down rapids and light enough to carry from one lake to the next.

The Indians of the Three Fires took pride in their canoes. In the warm seasons, the beautiful canoes were an important part of everyday life. Michigan Indians were always ready to paddle their canoes to places where they fished, hunted and traded.

But the lives of the Indians would soon change forever.

Far from the home of the Indians, in another part of the world, was a land called Europe. Separated by the huge Atlantic Ocean, the people living in the two different places knew nothing of each other.

In the year 1492, a man named Christopher Columbus sailed from Europe across the unknown Atlantic. Columbus returned to Europe with stories of a New World waiting beyond the waters.

The discoveries of Columbus caused great excitement in Europe. At the command of kings and queens and wealthy merchants, busy shipyards built fleets of wooden boats to carry the first Europeans to the far-away shores of the New World.

Many of the first explorers crossed the Atlantic Ocean in search of gold and silver. But to the poor and persecuted of Europe, the New World promised a greater wealth — a chance to start life over! Together they crowded on ships sailing for the New World.

Arriving on the distant shores, the Europeans rejoiced. The sweet smells of the dark forest and a curious, red-skinned people welcomed them ashore. The new land they called America appeared to be there for the taking.

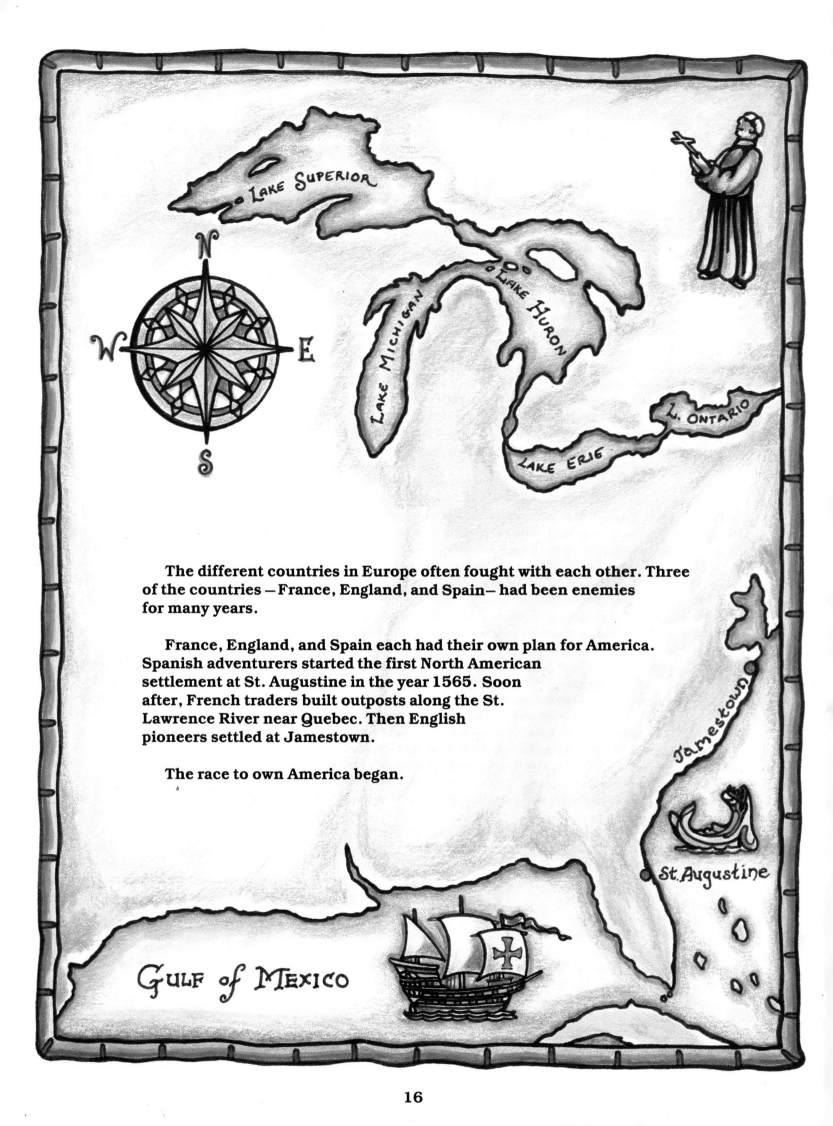

The different countries in Europe often fought with each other. Three of the countries—France, England, and Spain—had been enemies for many years.

France, England, and Spain each had their own plan for America. Spanish adventurers started the first North American settlement at St. Augustine in the year 1565. Soon after, French traders built outposts along the St. Lawrence River near Quebec. Then English pioneers settled at Jamestown.

The race to own America began.

The French were the first Europeans to reach Michigan.

Their journey from the Atlantic coast to Michigan began on the St. Lawrence River, where the waters of the distant Great Lakes emptied into the ocean. Travelling by canoe, the French were able to use the chain of lakes and rivers flowing to the ocean as a natural path to Michigan.

By the time the ship, the *Mayflower*, carried the first English pilgrims to Plymouth Rock, a French scout named Brulé had already seen Lake Superior and the Upper Peninsula of Michigan. Catholic missionaries followed Brulé's route to Michigan and preached to the Indian tribes they found living there.

The Indians were quick to see that many things made in France were superior to what they used. Metal kettles cooked better than clay pots. Rifles were deadlier than bows and arrows.

The Michigan wilderness was filled with fur-bearing animals, especially the sought-after beaver. In France, coats and hats made from the beautiful furs of animals trapped in Michigan were very popular.

Soon French merchants travelled deep into the Great Lakes country to trade with the Indians for furs.

The ship, the *Griffon*, built by the French explorer
La Salle to carry furs, was the first to sail the Great Lakes.

On her first voyage along the Michigan coast, the
Griffon was battered by strong winds and angry waves.
Somehow the sturdy ship survived.

After giving thanks, La Salle filled the
Griffon with furs. He ordered his crew
to sail the ship back east with her valuable cargo.
Then La Salle left the *Griffon* to explore
the wilderness on shore.

The *Griffon* sailed off into the horizon
and was never seen again. Nearly one hundred
years would pass before another sailing ship would
again brave the Great Lakes.

Deep in the Michigan wilderness, the fur trade grew quickly.

The Indians trapped beaver in the dead of winter, when the furs of the animals grew the thickest. In the spring, when icy rivers thawed, it was time to get the furs to market.

Bundles of furs were loaded into big canoes especially made for the fur trade. Rugged men called voyageurs paddled the heavy canoes from Michigan to far-away trading centers. Sometimes hundreds of canoes travelled together in caravans, and the songs and laughter of the voyageurs echoed through the quiet country.

For many years the forests of southern Michigan were swept by battles between the Algonquin Indians and their Iroquois Indian enemies. Fearing for their lives, few people dared to settle in the area.

Later, when the Indian tribes made peace, a Frenchman named Cadillac journeyed into the once-troubled land. In the year 1701, he built a log fort near the river flowing from Lake Huron to Lake Erie. Others followed Cadillac and settled close to the safety of the fort.

Cadillac named the growing town Detroit.

The French built the first settlements in Michigan. Working together with the Indians in the fur trade, the French ruled Michigan for over one hundred years.

But the English wanted the same things from Michigan as the French. Their traders competed for furs and their settlers moved toward land the French claimed.

In the year 1756, war broke out between the French and English in America. During the long struggle the English captured important French forts and cut off French outposts on the Great Lakes. Divided, the French surrendered.

Michigan became part of the English empire.

Angered by the way the English treated his people, an Indian, Chief Pontiac, plotted to force them out of Michigan.

Beneath the log walls of Fort Michilimackinac, clever Indian friends of Pontiac pretended to play a ball game. While English soldiers relaxed and watched the play, Indian women crept quietly into the fort with weapons hidden in their clothing. Suddenly the warriors attacked, surprising the English soldiers and capturing the fort.

But Pontiac could not defeat the English soldiers at Detroit. Discouraged, the Chief quit fighting and left Michigan.

To pay for the wars with the French and Indians, the English king demanded high taxes from the people living in America.

Americans did not like being taxed and ruled by distant England. They believed they could do better on their own. In the year 1776, American leaders signed the Declaration of Independence. No longer would Americans take orders from the English king. The Revolutionary War began.

The American George Washington and his rag-tag army fought against well-trained English troops. To the surprise of many, the Americans won. A new country, the United States of America, was born.

The peace treaty with England gave the United States the huge Northwest Territory. Laws passed to govern the wilderness territory encouraged settlement, education, and freedom.

Land was sold cheaply and most people could afford the price of a farm. Part of the money from the sale of land was set aside for building schools. Although allowed in other parts of the country, slavery in the Northwest Territory was forbidden.

As more and more people came to the Territory, the land was divided into five sections. One was named Michigan.

In the year 1812, England and the United States were again at war. The English attacked and quickly captured Michigan.

To supply their soldiers in Michigan, English ships needed to move freely on the Great Lakes. An American fleet commanded by Oliver Hazard Perry blocked their way. When Perry sighted English ships sailing down Lake Erie from Detroit, he attacked, and a day long battle began.

Perry's ship, the *Lawrence,* was splintered by cannon shot and scorched by fire. He changed ships, fought on, and won the fierce battle. Perry sent his commander the famous message, "We have met the enemy and they are ours..."

In the year 1820, the adventurous governor, Lewis Cass, set out on a long and dangerous journey to explore the unsettled Michigan Territory.

Travelling by canoe on the Great Lakes, Cass found Michigan to be much like it had been when roamed only by Indians. The empty coasts were darkened by ancient forests. The few Indians he met along the way had little contact with the outside world.

But in the coming years Michigan would change quickly. The quiet shores Cass travelled would soon fill with people.

The *Walk-in-the-Water* was the first steamship to come to Michigan. The strange smoky ship with splashing paddle wheels drew crowds wherever it docked. Driven by engines, steamships no longer needed sails and wind to move about. Soon dozens of steamships like the *Walk-in-the-Water* carried passengers between Great Lakes ports.

Improving transportation led to rapid settlement. The Erie Canal opened in the year 1825, making the trip to the Great Lakes from the Atlantic coast much easier. People came to the Michigan wilderness by the thousands seeking fertile land and a chance to make it on their own.

In the year 1837, Michigan joined the United States of America as the twenty-sixth state. Now Michigan was equal to all other states and shared in the strength of the growing nation.

Later, Lansing was chosen as the place to build Michigan's capitol. Government buildings rose from land that for centuries had been home only to the forest.

When Michigan became a state, it was forced to surrender a strip of land on its southern border to the state of Ohio. In return, Michigan was given a large part of the Upper Peninsula. Most people thought Michigan was cheated.

But five years later a geologist, Douglass Houghton, found rich deposits of copper in the Upper Peninsula. America's first great mining rush began. Then a mountain of iron was discovered near Marquette. Soon people praised the Upper Peninsula and the fortune in metals dug from the mines.

In the Upper Peninsula, at Sault Ste. Marie, the waters of Lake Superior fell twenty feet in wild rapids to the level of Lake Huron. Travel by ship through the rapids was impossible.

To solve the problem, special gates called locks were built to control the flow of water. Completed in the year 1855, the locks at Sault Ste. Marie gently carried ships from one lake level to another. Soon many ships brought iron and copper from Upper Peninsula mines to ports all along the Great Lakes.

Farmers slowly tamed Michigan's wilderness. Their axes cut into the thick forests and their plows turned the rich soil. The farmers' hard work was repaid with big crops.

Farming provided the people of Michigan with the necessities of life, and more. Homesteads grew from simple log shelters to fancy houses. Sailing ships carried Michigan farm crops to distant markets and returned full of merchandise.

The pioneers' dream of the good life in Michigan became a reality.

Transportation and communication improved as more and more settlers chose Michigan as home.

Big steam locomotives carrying passengers and cargo crossed the state. Horse-drawn wagons filled with pioneer families followed bumpy roads to the edge of the wilderness. Towns sprang up at crossroads and at stops along the railroad tracks.

Telegraph and postal service linked the towns, and newspapers helped keep the people of Michigan informed.

The Civil War was a sad time for all of America.

The nation split in the fight over slavery, North against South. President Abraham Lincoln called on northern states to hold the United States together. Michigan stood behind Lincoln and sent soldiers and supplies to help keep the United States one nation.

Over 90,000 Michigan volunteers fought in the long Civil War. Many died. Many more were wounded. But the sacrifices of Michigan soldiers helped pull the nation back together and forever end slavery in the United States.

During the Civil War the first big factories were built in Michigan. Iron and copper mined in the Upper Peninsula were shipped to ports in the southern part of the state, where the factories turned the metals into products needed to win the war.

Steam engines, railroad cars, iron wheels, even soldiers' brass buttons, were made in Michigan. Later the same Michigan products helped rebuild the war-torn country.

To the pioneer farmers, the forests of Michigan were a nuisance. The huge trees had to be cut to let in light for crops. But when settlers rushed to Michigan after the Civil War, people were willing to pay for the wood needed to build new towns. Lumberjacks invaded Michigan forests.

The biggest white pine trees in the world grew in Michigan. Bunched close together they darkened the forest floor. The lumber from one of the giant trees could build a whole house.

The wood of the white pine was famous for being straight, strong, and light. The white pines were the first trees to fall to the lumberjack's ax.

Trees were cut in the winter when the slippery snow and ice made heavy logs easier to move. In the spring, huge piles of logs were dumped in the nearest river. Lumberjacks rode on the bobbing logs, steering them around bends and freeing them from snags. It was a dangerous job.

Behind floated the wanigan, the cook house where a meal was always ready for hungry workers.

The mills waited downriver. One by one the logs were fed to the whining saws. High stacks of cut lumber crowded the docks, ready for shipment to ports throughout the country.

Saginaw, Michigan's first big lumber town, for years sawed more wood than any place in the world. Across the state, Grand Rapids became famous for making wood furniture. Other towns grew quickly as the lumberjacks cut their way north to the next stand of timber.

Many people believed the forests of Michigan would last forever. But by the year 1900, almost all of Michigan's trees had been cut. Towns dependent on lumber for their livelihood withered and died.

Throughout the lumbering days, farmers moved on to the land cleared when the trees were cut. At the turn of the century, most people in Michigan lived on farms. But new jobs in factories brought more and more people to Michigan cities.

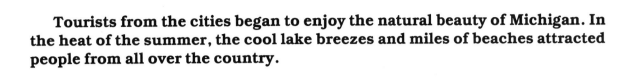

Tourists from the cities began to enjoy the natural beauty of Michigan. In the heat of the summer, the cool lake breezes and miles of beaches attracted people from all over the country.

Loaded with vacationers, paddle-wheeled ships steamed up the Great Lakes to resort towns all along the Michigan shoreline.

Henry Ford began making the Model T automobile in Detroit in
the year 1909. While others made cars one at a time, Ford forever
changed the rules of manufacturing by using the assembly line.

On the assembly line, many cars were put together at once from
parts that were exactly alike. Workers made cars more quickly and
at less cost than before. The automobile, once considered a toy for
the rich, could now be purchased by many people.

Almost overnight Michigan led the world in manufacturing.

42

Mass production of the automobile forever changed Michigan. The promise of high paying jobs brought in people from all over the world. Skyscrapers shot up and towns spread out.

The nation, too, was changed. Highways were improved, and people could travel between places at speeds never before imagined. A trip that used to take a day could now be made in hours.

The pace of life quickened.

In the year 1957 the Mackinaw Bridge was completed, linking the Upper and Lower Peninsulas of Michigan. The bridge, famous for its beauty and strength, stands as a sturdy tribute to the state that for many years led the world in manufacturing.

Michigan has a rich and colorful past. The Indians and fur traders, the miners and lumberjacks, the farmers and auto workers, all left their mark on the state.

Guided by the lessons of the past, and with dreams and courage of their own, the children of a new generation will write tomorrow's stories of the special place called Michigan.